WENDY UNWRITTEN

Kat Ramsburg

BROADWAY PLAY PUBLISHING INC
New York
www.broadwayplaypub.com
info@broadwayplaypub.com

WENDY UNWRITTEN
© Copyright 2020 Kat Ramsburg

First edition: November 2020
I S B N: 978-0-88145-884-8

Book design: Marie Donovan
Page make-up: Adobe InDesign
Typeface: Palatino

WENDY UNWRITTEN was commissioned by
Acadiana Repertory Theatre in Lafayette, Louisiana.
and developed by the Great Plains Theatre Conference.

WENDY UNWRITTEN received its Developmental
Premiere at Acadiana Repertory Theatre (Artistic
Director, Steven Landry) on 14 July 2017. The cast and
creative contributors were:

WENDY .... Debbie Ardoin
JOHN .... Steven R Landry
MICHAEL .... Allen Higginbotham
JANE ....Erica Jure
BOY .... Conner Vaccaro

Director.. Gabe Ortego

CHARACTERS

WENDY, *early/mid 60's. A gifted storyteller. Her life was planned out for her, but now that she's free, she's both excited by and terrified of the possibilities.*

JOHN, *40. Uptight. Neurotic. Believes in the patriarchy.*
Also plays: CAPTAIN

MICHAEL, *39. Fun loving, lacking inhibitions, wears his heart on his sleeve.*
(Please note: MICHAEL *is childlike, not childish. Think Lost Boy.)*

JANE, *32. A feminist through and through and will fight to the death for gender parity, a woman's right to choose, and toppling the patriarchy.*
Also plays: BELLE

BOY, *12. Energetic and scrappy. There's nothing precocious or cute about him. Find the most rambunctious boy on the playground, and teach him to deliver lines.*

The play allows for diverse casting. It takes place in Seattle, where there is a rich tapestry of ethnicities, particularly Black, Latinx, Asian Americans, and Indigenous people. Please make every effort to reflect this diversity in your casting.

SETTING

Time: Present
Place: Ballard, Washington & Never Neverland

A NOTE ON DESIGN

There are a number of magical elements in this play, all of which can be accomplished with a budget of five, five thousand, or five million dollars! (If you're doing a five million dollar production of this play, please send pictures!)

Imagination is key here, not a hefty budget.

Wendy Grew Up

(The suggested living room of a modest middle class home, when there was still such a thing as a middle class. There are three walls, maybe not even fully realized. These walls will dismantle over the course of the play, as WENDY's *life is also dismantled.)*

(But in the current living room, with all three walls intact, sit JANE, WENDY, MICHAEL *and* JOHN, *in precisely that order. They are perched on four short stools that face out to the audience. The family is sitting Shiva.)*

(A clock ticks loudly. Time is passing.)

*(*JOHN *inconspicuously checks his watch.)*

*(*JANE *smells her pits.)*

*(*MICHAEL *starts to loosen his tie.)*

WENDY: Don't you dare—

MICHAEL: It's really hot in here.

WENDY: It's really hot in hell too.

JANE: Jews don't believe in hell.

MICHAEL: They don't?

JOHN: How would you know? How would any of us know?

JANE: Cultural awareness?

WENDY: Your father was Jewish and wanted us to sit Shiva for him, so we're sitting Shiva.

JOHN: Father was hardly Jewish.

MICHAEL: He didn't wear one of those... What's it —
tiny hats?

Yam? Yammy...

JANE: Yarmulke.

MICHAEL: Yeah. Or the thing with the strings.

JANE: Prayer shawl.

JOHN: We get it. You've seen *Fiddler on the Roof.*

WENDY: He wasn't that kind of Jew.

MICHAEL: What kind was he?

JOHN: He was the kind of Jew who never, ever, once in
his life mentioned being Jewish.

WENDY: Maybe you didn't know him as well as you
thought?

JOHN: He was my best friend.

WENDY: Kids think they know everything about their
parents but really—

JOHN: He would have mentioned if he was Jewish.

WENDY: His Jewishness was very important to him as a
child, but then he grew up and he wasn't as—

JANE: Naïve?

WENDY: The mysticism. Something didn't sit well with
him.

JOHN: But at sixty-five he decided it was important
again?

WENDY: I believed in lots of things when I was a kid
that I don't believe in now.

MICHAEL: Like Santa?

JOHN: I never believed in Santa.

WENDY: Oh yes you did.

JOHN: I did not.

WENDY: I have a V H S around here somewhere of you sobbing because you had asked Santa for some of those Garbage Bucket Kids—

JOHN: Garbage *Pail* Kids.

WENDY: Those awful cards! Santa didn't bring them because they were trash, and you threw the biggest fit I've ever seen.

MICHAEL: I remember that!

JOHN: I *knew* there was no Santa and was mad at *you* and *dad* for not getting them.

WENDY: I remember very clearly. You said, "If Santa can't be bothered to bring me the *one* thing I asked for, I reject all of his gifts."

MICHAEL: So mom packed up the rest of the gifts up and took them to the homeless shelter. He didn't get anything that year.

WENDY: All over some ridiculous Garbage Bucket—

JOHN: *PAIL*—and anyway, I'm just not clear on how this story proves anything. Father is dead. Us sitting Shiva doesn't make him more Jewish. And it certainly doesn't make *us* Jewish.

JANE: Even if dad was Jewish, you have to come out of a Jewish vagina to be Jewish and you're not Jewish, right mom?

MICHAEL: How 'bout any time anyone says "Jewish" we down some Manischewitz.

WENDY: You don't have to be a Jew to sit Shiva.

JANE: I'm pretty sure you do.

WENDY: When we're done here, you can Google it and find out.

MICHAEL: I've got my phone—
(*He starts to pull his phone from his pocket.*)

WENDY: No devices.

(MICHAEL *puts it back.*)

WENDY: No T V.

MICHAEL: Whaaaaat?!

WENDY: No shaving—

JOHN: Should be easy for Jane.

JANE: You don't shave your pits, why should I shave mine?

JOHN: It's standard grooming for a lady.

JANE: And I reject your *standards*.

JOHN: If you ever have any hope of marrying—

JANE: Oh. My. Gosh! / When are you going to—

JOHN: *(Overlapping)* I'm just saying—	MICHAEL: *(Overlapping)* I've really got to pee.
JANE: I *know* what you're saying.	
JOHN: You wonder why you're alone.	Like really, really bad.
JANE: I have literally never wondered that.	I'm pretty sure my bladder is about to burst and my penis will explode.

JOHN: *(To* MICHAEL*)* That's not how penises work. *(To* JANE*)* And you're not exactly the commitment type.

JANE: Who says I want commitment? Maybe I just want sex.	MICHAEL: I'll be right back.

(MICHAEL *stands.*)

WENDY: You sit down. And you two shut up.

MICHAEL: I've got to pee.

WENDY: You'll pee when it's over. Sit. Down.

(MICHAEL *sits.*)

WENDY: Your father left detailed instructions on how he wanted to be remembered. This is the last request he will ever have of you, and it will not kill you to indulge him.

And if it does kill you, that's fine, because we're already sitting Shiva for one member of this family. We might as well make it two.

Now sit still and shut up.

Johnny, read this.

(WENDY *hands* JOHN *a card with a prayer printed on it.*)

JOHN: It's in Hebrew.

WENDY: Turn it over.

JOHN: "Exalted and hallowed be God's great name, in the world, which God created—"
I thought Jews don't say "God."

JANE: They don't spell "God" but they can say it.

MICHAEL: How would they know when to say it, if they don't write it down?

JANE: They write "g", "d".

MICHAEL: God damn?

WENDY:	JANE:	JOHN:
Michael!	You're an idiot!	Seriously?

JANE: G *dash* d.

MICHAEL: But if that still stands for God, why not just write God?

WENDY: It's sacred.

MICHAEL: That doesn't make any sense.

JOHN: It doesn't matter if it doesn't make sense to you. You're not Jewish. I'm not Jewish. Mother and Jane aren't Jewish.

We're not Jewish!

(Pause. WENDY *checks her watch.)*

MICHAEL: So... What now?

WENDY: We wait, Michael.
People will come pay their respects. We will graciously accept them.
And in seven days we'll—

JOHN: You didn't tell   JANE: *SEVEN* days
me *seven days.*

MICHAEL: I cannot hold my pee for seven days.

WENDY: Shiva's are seven days. At least that's what I read on—
(She pulls out a piece of paper from her bra. A Wiki How: How to Sit Shiva print out from the internet.)
—Yup. Seven days. Apparently when it's over, we are healed.

MICHAEL: Healed from what?

JOHN: From our grief.

WENDY: If that's what you're feeling.

JANE: Isn't that what you're feeling?

JOHN: Of course mother is grieving. We're *all* grieving.

MICHAEL: I'm not grieving.

JOHN: How can you say that?

MICHAEL: It's the truth.

JOHN: You don't know what you're feeling.

JANE: Then by all means, tell us what we're feeling.

JOHN: Our *father* is dead. The leader of this family is *dead*. We are a team without a coach!

A ship without a captain!

JANE: A circus without a ringleader.

MICHAEL: Antarctica without a polar bear!

(*Everyone looks at* MICHAEL *in confusion.*)

MICHAEL: Because the polar bears are dead.

WENDY: We're free.

(*Everyone looks at* WENDY. *What did she say?*)

JOHN: I'm sorry?

WENDY: I said, we're free.
Free.
All of us. Free.

JANE: Free of what?

WENDY: This…pretense.

JOHN: What pretense?

WENDY: This house.
Our life.
This is the best thing that could have happened to us.
We can be anything we want to be now.

JOHN: We'll be the same as we've always been.

WENDY: I'm not interested in that.

JOHN: We don't have much of a choice, Mother. Our lives are already in progress. Everything is planned out.

WENDY: I'm sure Sylvie and the twins would agree with you, but I've done my time.

JOHN: Is that how you see our life? Just putting in time?

WENDY: Some days. Yes.

MICHAEL: What do you want to do now?

WENDY: I—

I think I might—

(Long pause of anticipation)

JANE: How about a cooking class? You could learn to make those macaroon things.

JOHN: Maca*ron*. Not Macaroon. Completely different thing.

JANE: I know the difference, John!

JOHN: You said Maca*roon*. Mother likes maca*rons*.

WENDY: I hate them actually.

JANE: No, you don't!

WENDY: I find them pretentious.

JANE: But I always send them to you for Mother's Day.

WENDY: Yes you do.

MICHAEL: They're delicious.

JANE: Seriously? A box of macaroons is like thirty dollars! You let *him* eat them?

WENDY: I don't like them.

MICHAEL: I love them. Not the pistachio though. Uglch! Gag me.

JANE: Mom!

WENDY: I. Don't. Like. Them.

JOHN: Sylvie took a class on floral design once. I could get the name of the place from her.

Or maybe you could take a class together!

WENDY: I would rather eat pesticides while sitting naked on a bed of nails.

JOHN: You just need to get to know her—

WENDY: You've been married to her for 14 years.

JANE: I think it would be good for you to have an activity.
Something to look forward to.
Get you out of the house.

WENDY: I have many things I'm looking forward to, Jane. Your father's death does not mean my death. I am someone without him by my side.

JANE: I wasn't implying—

WENDY: I know what you all think of me. But you're wrong. You've been wrong for many, many years.

JOHN: We think the world of you, Mother.

WENDY: And stop calling me mother. It's obnoxious. Always has been.

JOHN: But that's what you are.

WENDY: My name is Wendy.
Not "Mother, mamma, mom, mommy, grandma, wifey, my old lady…"
Wendy.
And I like my name, so try using it.

MICHAEL: Wen-dy.
Feels weird.

JANE: Whatever you want, Mom—Wendy.

WENDY: (*Looking at her watch*) Well, it's been seventeen minutes. What do you say we call it good?

(MICHAEL *jumps to his feet, and runs out of the room, presumably to pee.*)

JANE: What happened to seven days?

WENDY: I gave your father forty-one years of my life. I don't regret all of those years, but—
I've got a lot of living to do.

JOHN: *Regret?* Is my entire childhood a lie?

WENDY: Calm down, John. This isn't about you.

JOHN: Well it's certainly not about father.

WENDY: The last forty-one years have been about him. It's time for a change.

JOHN: Him being gone is a big enough change.

WENDY: Don't you think it's a sign that the first thought I had when the doctor came out to tell me he hadn't made it was, "I'm free".

JOHN: You were in shock.

JANE: No one thought he was going to die.

WENDY: He knew.

JOHN: There's no way he could have.

WENDY: I'm telling you.
Two nights ago, your father and I sat on this couch. The rain was pouring down. There was a feisty wind. Branches banging against the windows. You couldn't have imagined a more appropriate setting for your father to tell me he had a bad feeling about the surgery. He wanted to go through all the paperwork. I kept saying, "This is ridiculous. It's a hip replacement." But your father is your father and likes...*liked* things taken care of, and so he said, "Prepare for the worst."

(MICHAEL *flops on the couch and starts playing a game on his phone. We hear the obnoxious electronic music from the game.*)

JOHN: Nice. Real nice.

MICHAEL: What? Shiva's over.

JOHN: That doesn't mean you can throw decency out the window.
We are *mourning.*

MICHAEL: I'm not. I don't miss dad at all.

JOHN: At all?

JANE: John, don't start.

JOHN: He's talking about my father.

JANE: *Our* father. And Michael has every right to mourn or not mourn.

JOHN: He was a *good* man.

MICHAEL: He was mean!

JOHN: He was *hard* on you. There's a difference.

MICHAEL: The difference being, he was *mean* to me because he loved you more.

JANE: Guys, let's not.

MICHAEL: I'm just glad he died and not mom.

JOHN: Because father would have made you get off the couch and make something of yourself.

JANE: John! Stop it.

JOHN: You are lazy and irresponsible.

MICHAEL: I am an artist. I'm not a bad person. Mom, tell John I'm not a bad person! Tell John I'm not a bad person!

JANE: John, Michael. Stop! This isn't the time.

JOHN: And to sit there and speak ill of him!

WENDY: (*Making the decision right then and there.*) I'm going to sell the house.

JANE: What are you saying?

MICHAEL: You can't. This is our home!

JOHN: No! That's not a rational—

WENDY: Yes. I'm going to sell the house. I don't want it.

MICHAEL: Where will I live?

WENDY: You'll figure it out.

JOHN: But the girls love coming here for Christmas!

WENDY: Life's full of disappointment. Start 'em young.

JANE: Where will you live?

(WENDY *looks at* JANE *then* JOHN.)

(After a beat)

WENDY: Don't all jump in to invite me to live with you after I've given up my entire life taking care of you.

JANE:	JOHN:	MICHAEL:
It's just I live in	The girls have	
a studio and—	their own rooms	I live here…
	now so—	

WENDY: Oh, calm down. I don't want to live with you any more than you want to live with me.
I'll call the realtor in the morning.

JOHN: Maybe we should take some time to think about it.

Make a decision after we've had time to process all of this…

WENDY: It's not your decision to make.

JOHN: It's part of our inheritance.

WENDY: I'm not dead yet. It's still mine.

JOHN: Father is the one who worked for it. I would argue that—

WENDY: Consider it payment for the year I spent raising you three, doing his laundry, making his meals, keeping his life in order so he could go out and make a living.

MICHAEL: But what will we do for money when you're gone?

WENDY: Get a job, pumpkin.

MICHAEL: I have a job.

JOHN: Get one that pays a salary. Insurance. 401k.

MICHAEL: I'm not selling my soul to the corporate
overlords so I can turn out like you.
I've made a commitment to my art.

WENDY: And that's fine baby, but that doesn't mean it's
my job to make up for your decision. I let you live here
because I like having you around, but it's time to move
on.

MICHAEL: Why can't I go where you go?

WENDY: Because I don't know where I'm going yet.

JOHN: Shouldn't you think about that before you sell
the house?

WENDY: It will work itself out.
Ha! I like that.
"It will work itself out."

JANE: Mom. I'm worried about you making big
decisions right now. Dad died two days ago. There's
no rush.

(WENDY *takes in each of her kids.*)

WENDY: Come here. All of you.

(*They settle in on the couch, as they probably did as
children.*)

WENDY: You don't know this about me, but I used to
be someone remarkable. I had ambition, and dreams,
and a sense of adventure. But my father and mother
believed I had too much ambition and too many
dreams. They knew the world I lived in was not
welcoming to imaginative, daring girls. So instead of
encouraging me to change the world, they taught me to
adapt to it. I learned to have no opinions other than the

opinions my father had, and then my husband. I was
raised to be quiet and kind, considerate and helpful.
But the world has changed — at least it feels like it
has. And I just want to see what the world holds for
someone like me.
So I'm selling the house.
And frankly, I don't care what any of you think about
that.

(Transition)

An Afterthought

(WENDY steps into a pool of light.)

(The clock stops ticking.)

WENDY: Once upon a time…
When I was a girl,
my mother read me the story of another little girl,
who shared my name.
In this story, the little girl followed a boy because he
asked her to.
He said, "come with me, and I'll show you the most
magical place you could ever imagine."
And so she went.

The boy was right. The place was magical.
Wendy loved it there.
Truth be told, she also loved the boy.
She wanted to do anything to prove to the boy that she
should stay there with him.
So she cooked for him. And cleaned his home. And
mended his socks.
Not just for him, but for all of his friends too. And the
boy, instead of saying thank you, or understanding
what Wendy was trying to say with her actions…
Instead the boy kept running outside to play with the
other boys.

And Wendy was left in the house.
Alone.

She tried to tell him how she felt,
That she had lost herself, somehow.
In him.
In that place.
But Wendy learned that a girl's words often fall on
deaf ears.
So she quietly continued to cook, clean, and mend.
And the boy remained oblivious.
And Wendy became sad.

Very, very sad.

Occasionally she'd get to go on an adventure, but it
usually ended with her rescuing the boys,
and the boys thinking they had saved her.

That's the part I remember most vividly.

Eventually Wendy returned to her family,
But for the rest of her life, Wendy pined for the boy.
She wondered what had become of him?
Did he ever grow up?
Did he eventually succumb to the idea that life isn't all
about being gay and innocent?
But rather, about letting every bit of childlike wonder
slip away from you,
one laugh at a time.

Until you no longer remember laughing at all.

(Transition)

Wendy And John

*(WENDY sits on the couch, taking apart a Pirate's Ship built
with Legos.)*

(The clock is ticking.)

(JOHN *comes through the front door without knocking.*)

JOHN: What are you—? Don't do that! Father and I—

WENDY: I thought the girls would like to rebuild it with you.

(JOHN *picks up the individual pieces.*)

JOHN: Oh! Oh no! No, no, no! It's…destroyed.

WENDY: You haven't touched it since you first put it together with your dad.

JOHN: Because we finished it. It was complete.

WENDY: It was collecting dust. Legos are toys. Not sculptures.

JOHN: I was proud of it.

WENDY: I'll bag up the pieces for you and the girls.

JOHN: You could have asked me what I wanted to do with it.

WENDY: It's been sitting here like a monument to your childhood.

JOHN: That seems reasonable, as this is my childhood home.

WENDY: The house is on the market. We have to clean things out. You can take anything you'd like, but you have to take it today. Otherwise it goes to charity.

JOHN: We need to take time to consider our options.

WENDY: *My* options Johnny.

JOHN: You don't have to call me Johnny anymore. Dad's not around.

WENDY: You'll always be my Johnny.

JOHN: It's so juvenile.

WENDY: Imagine that! You were a little boy when we started calling you that.

JOHN: And now I'm a man. And John Sr. is dead. So
please—

WENDY: Alright. Okay.
So the Legos—

(JOHN *whisks away the remains of the pirate ship.*)

JOHN: Just—please. Leave it be.

(WENDY *slides the loose pieces into a Ziplock bag.*)

WENDY: We should go through your books while
you're here. We can donate the ones you don't want to
the library. Unless you think the girls—

JOHN: Mother. Stop. There's no rush.

WENDY: Oh but there is.
I have so much to do.
So much to be.

JOHN: I didn't come by to go through my belongings.
I've brought the two offers from the realtor.

WENDY: Oh. Right.

JOHN: Now, this one is lower, but it's in cash. The
higher one is financed and dependent on the buyer
selling their current home.

WENDY: I didn't think we'd get offers so quickly.

JOHN: I told you to think this through before you listed
the house.

WENDY: It feels like maybe the cash offer is the way to
go?

JOHN: See Mother, the thing is, it's a real nice family
that is giving you the higher offer.
The cash offer—that's a developer who wants to tear
the place down and build multi-family condos.

WENDY: That's not a bad idea actually.

JOHN: It's a terrible idea. This is a perfectly decent home for a young family.

WENDY: So why don't you buy it?

JOHN: I thought about it.

Talked to Sylvie, but, well…

WENDY: Not her taste.

JOHN: It's just—the schools in our neighborhood are—

WENDY: The schools here are fine.

JOHN: Yes, they're fine. But Juniper and Willow, they need something more challenging.

WENDY: Oh please, Juniper's not bright. And Willow—well you can make a case there, but Juniper…

Good thing she's the pretty one.

JOHN: They're identical.

WENDY: Does Willow's nose know that?

JOHN: Sylvie says it's fixable. When she's older.

And anyway, Sylvie wants to keep the girls in their school. It's too far of a drive from here.

WENDY: So you'll stay in your big old fancy house, locked away with other fancy houses, behind a fancy gate to keep out god-knows-what.

JOHN: It's a safety precaution.

WENDY: Don't you ever wonder what you're keeping out? What if the best things that could possibly happen to you lie just beyond that gate?

JOHN: Don't be fantastical Mother.

WENDY: Oh but I am John.

Do you remember when we came to look at this house?

JOHN: I was five.

WENDY: Five year olds have memories.

JOHN: Well I don't remember, but I'm sure you have a slightly unbelievable story about how you knew this house contained magic from the moment you walked in.

WENDY: Ah. So you *do* remember.
We had seen probably thirty houses—five that day alone. You and Michael were exhausted and behaving like little jerks.

JOHN: Mother.

WENDY: What? You were. *You* in particular were a giant asshole when you were hungry or tired.

Never really did outgrow that, did you?

JOHN: I'm hypoglycemic.

WENDY: We walked into this house—the last one of the day. And something...

JOHN: "Magical happened."

WENDY: *(Slightly overlapping)* —*Magical* happened. All of our energy returned. Our faces became flush with the warmth of pure joy. You and Michael charged up the stairs to choose your bedroom.
Your dad and I looked at the kitchen, the dining room, the den that would become his office... And while he discussed the details with the realtor, I snuck upstairs to see what you boys were up to. Do you know what I found?

JOHN: I assume Michael was crying over something.

WENDY: I found the two of you, side by side, looking out the big bay window in your bedroom. You were pointing out the stars to Michael. Identifying them for him. You were so patient. So wise.
It was the first moment I thought, "Ah yes, they are brothers now".
And I knew this was our house.

JOHN: Father said he got a good deal on it. That's why he chose it.

WENDY: Oh we did! But it's because I told the former owners I knew the house contained magic and I would honor the magic to the best of my ability. They loved that I saw everything this house was and cut the price so we could afford it.

JOHN: That story feels a little unrealistic, don't you think?

(Beat)

WENDY: What happened John? When you were doing flips in my womb, I thought you might be part mermaid. I dreamed of the adventures we'd have — the places we'd go. Swimming in Antarctica. Picnics on Mars.

JOHN: Nothing *happened.* I simply thrive on order and responsibility.
I take great pride in providing for my family.

WENDY: But what if there was something else you could take pride in?

JOHN: *(Annoyed at this line of questioning)* Like what?

WENDY: What else interests you?

JOHN: What do you mean?

WENDY: What would you do if you had a day free? All to yourself. No wife, no kids.

Come on! Try to imagine it. I know your imagination is in there somewhere.

JOHN: I...
I would...
I guess I'd try to get to inbox zero.

WENDY: Oh, Johnny! I pity the life you lead.

JOHN: I'm doing perfectly fine.

WENDY: No you're not. You want to believe you're happy so that your life makes sense.

JOHN: No, Mother. I've just learned that happiness isn't necessarily a requirement to keep moving forward in life.
There are highs and lows, and one must face each day without fully giving in to either one. "Slow and steady wins the race," as they say.

WENDY: How about looking for a little magic every day? It's there. In the highs and the lows.

(JOHN *scoffs*.)

WENDY: It's in the way a grocery bagger wishes you good day as she hands you your groceries. In the way the sun sneaks out from behind a cloud to remind you it's always there. It's in the secret language the twins use with each other.

JOHN: That's just nonsense. Babble, really.

WENDY: Oh darling.

JOHN: If there's so much magic in your world, why do you act like life with Father was so difficult?

WENDY: Don't put words in my mouth. It was never difficult.
Your father decided that order and responsibility took precedent over magic. I disagreed.
It was challenging.
I began to doubt myself, my being, my purpose.
I lost my way.
All I want to do it find it again.
…You could come with me.

JOHN: You don't really want me to come.

WENDY: Oh but I do!
Together we could climb trees! Hunt crocodiles!

JOHN: But Sylvie. And the girls…

WENDY: We'll come back… eventually.
Come with me, Johnny.
See what you've been missing.
Let me show you what it's like to let your shoulders
drop—to let yourself go free.

JOHN: I — I *want* to…

WENDY: Then do.

JOHN: I just don't know if—

WENDY: You can.

JOHN: Or how?

WENDY: I'll show you.

JOHN: But my responsibilities—

WENDY: —will wait, while you swim with the
mermaids!

(JOHN *takes* WENDY *in. For a moment he is lost in this
possibility, but then…*)

JOHN: No. No, no, no, no. You're doing it again. You're
trying to turn me into someone I'm not. Someone more
like Michael. Someone foolish and impractical.

WENDY: I've simply invited you to come with me.
What happens when we get there is up to you.

JOHN: Every day I wake up. I brush my teeth. I go
down to the basement for forty-five minutes of cardio.
I come upstairs. I make the coffee. I take the coffee
upstairs. I wake Sylvie and the girls. I take a shower.
I come downstairs to eat breakfast with my family.
I drive to work. I clock in. I clock out. I drive home.
We eat dinner as a family. Sylvie, the girls and I do an
activity. Maybe we go on a walk. Perhaps we watch a
documentary. The girls brush their teeth. We put them
to bed. I catch up on work emails. I brush my teeth. I
go to bed. Every. Single. Day.

It's what I like. It's how Sylvie and I maintain control. It's how I know that the chaos of this world will not penetrate my family.
Sylvie and I will live happily ever after. My children will achieve all that they can achieve. And whatever's happening out there—out where sadness, and violence, and illness, and anger destroy people's lives—that will not affect *my* family.

WENDY: We all like to believe in things that can't possibly be true.

JOHN: Just stop. Please stop making me feel as though my choices mean I'm stuck, or too conservative, or lack spontaneity. Stop making me believe that I'm not enough. And stop pretending there's a magical land where the pressures I put on myself for my family don't exist.
And there's no such thing as a mermaid!

WENDY: How would you know?

JOHN: Because logically—

WENDY: You've never looked for them.

JOHN: *Scientifically*—there is no possible way for—

WENDY: Just because you haven't seen something doesn't mean you can't *imagine* it to be so. You're too focused on what's *proven*, but what about what's still out there to be discovered? Wouldn't it be incredible to discover something that everyone else thought was impossible? Wouldn't it be lovely to dream again?

JOHN: I want to live in the present.
I have no need to hide away in fantasies.
Imagination is for those who are not strong enough to handle reality.

WENDY: Imagination is for those who are not *content* with reality.

JOHN: What is so wrong with our life that you *need* to escape it?

WENDY: Nothing is wrong with this life John.
Except I know it's not the one I was meant to live.
There's a bigger life for me out there.
And I'm going to find it.
You wish that I could see your life as desirable
And I wish you could see my choice as a valid one.
You are not going to limit my dreams.
Or make me feel like I'm betraying this life while searching for the one that was meant to be mine.
Take the cash offer. I want out of this house as soon as possible.
Where do I sign?

(JOHN *pulls a pen from his jacket.*)

JOHN: Can we at least think on it for a day?

(WENDY *takes the pen and signs the contract.*)

WENDY: You are not the first man to try to wrangle me, but you will be the last.

(*One side of the house falls away.*)

(*Transition*)

Wendy And Jane

(The house is filled with boxes, and garbage bags. Most of the boxes are marked "Goodwill." There is a small stack marked "storage."

(*The clock ticks away.*)

(JANE *is taping up boxes, while* WENDY *goes through things on a bookcase.*)

(WENDY *hands* JANE *a trophy.*)

WENDY: Trash.

Wait.
No.

JANE: Maybe storage?

WENDY: Yes. Good idea.

No. Trash.

JANE: But it's Dad's.
Why don't we put all of this in storage until you figure things out?

WENDY: I'm thinking maybe just get rid of it all?
Is that crazy?

JANE: A little.
I don't want you to regret—

WENDY: No. No more regrets.
(Making the decision)
Toss it all.

JANE: Mom…

WENDY: You've had a couple of weeks to process this, but I've had forty-one years.
I don't want that trophy. I don't want any of this stuff.
It does not spark joy.

JANE: You've really been dreaming of this day that long?

WENDY: Not every day.
Not every year.

JANE: You were so good at hiding it.

WENDY: Oh, I don't know about that.

JANE: I never saw it.
Your distaste for this life. Raising us. Being married.
You seemed like the perfect housewife.
I hated that about you.

WENDY: And boy did you let me know it.
All your rants about housewives, and how you would
never let your brain rot away like that.
Leaving copies of *Fear of Flying* and *The Feminist
Mystique* lying around when all your other books were
so carefully catalogued in your room.
I'm smarter than you give me credit for.
I enjoyed *The Feminist Mystique* by the way.

JANE: You read it?

WENDY: Long before you were born.
You didn't invent feminism, you know.

JANE: But if you read them why didn't you—

WENDY: They felt like they were for someone else.
Someone more bold than I ever was.
I discovered some books I hadn't read, in your room
when you went off to college.
The Second Sex.
Diary of a Mad Housewife.
I'm guessing you left those for me to find as well?

(JANE *doesn't have to answer that question.*)

WENDY: Those books gave me comfort.
I wasn't the only one who had made the wrong
decision.

JANE: Do you really see it that way?

WENDY: I'll never know who I could have been.
Or see the places I should have seen.
And who knows?
Maybe had I done all of that first, I wouldn't have
screwed you kids up as much as I did.

JANE: You didn't screw us up.

WENDY: John would disagree with you.

JANE: We turned out fine mom.

We each got a different version of you, and you got
three radically different kids but...
We're all okay.

WENDY: I loved you all equally.

JANE: Yeah.
But differently.

WENDY: You guys talk about this? Compare my love?

JANE: The three of us—have a healthy conversation?
Hell no.
You got married because you were knocked up with
John.
Michael was a surprise, but you made it work.
Then I showed up a few years later.
An accident.

WENDY: You were wanted.

JANE: I was *welcome*, but not necessarily *wanted*.

WENDY: Your father was delighted to finally have a
girl.

JANE: Yeah...
I just don't think *you* were prepared for one.

WENDY: I didn't know anything about girls. I grew up
with brothers!
But I loved you.

JANE: But why didn't you—
You never *tried* with me, you know?
Like—okay this is a weird example—we never baked
together.
But you bake with Juniper and Willow all the time.

WENDY: You want to bake?
We can bake!
The cookie sheets are in one of these boxes.

JANE: Mom. No. Not now.

Then. I wanted to bake *then.*

WENDY: You could have said something.

JANE: You could have asked.

WENDY: When were you home to ask?

JANE: I would have gladly stayed home if it meant hanging out with you.

WENDY: You say that now. But I remember a girl who was pretty adamant that her mother was "so lame." You made me drop you off a block from school.
I wasn't allowed to meet your friends.
You were ashamed of me.

JANE: I was not.

WENDY: Oh, you were.

JANE: Okay, yeah. Maybe in high school.
All the other moms…
I just didn't know any moms whose only job was to care for their husband and kids.
Like, you had nothing else to talk about, because you didn't do anything else.
The other moms were lawyers, and tennis players, and Girl Scout Leaders.
You were just…mom.

WENDY: That's what your father wanted me to be.

JANE: I see that now.
But back then I thought it was your choice, and I resented it.
And you.
And…
I vowed to never become what you were.

WENDY: Little did you know I vowed the same thing for you.

JANE: You did?

WENDY: Oh yes. I wanted the world for you.
Still do.

JANE: But you never—
You were so hands off with me.

WENDY: I made sure you had a mind of your own.
I taught you to speak up when your brothers were
louder than you.
You were given every opportunity the boys were
given, and then some.
I made sure you never had different expectations
placed on you because of your gender.

JANE: Why didn't you want those things for yourself?

WENDY: You think I didn't?
Then where did I get the idea to raise you the way I
did?

(Beat)

JANE: I'm so sorry.
And now…
Ugh.
This is terrible.

WENDY: What is?
This?
No. I'll be fine. I'll be more than fine.

JANE: Not you.
Me.
I'm…pregnant.

WENDY: Oh.

JANE: The dad is this guy I kind of sleep with, when
I'm in between things with this other guy that I have
an on again off again thing with.

WENDY: *(Not following)* Okay…

JANE: But he's a *boy*. If I'm going to raise a kid, I want it to be with a *man*.
But they don't seem to exist. At least not at my age.
It's like it takes them ten years longer than women to realize they're on their own, that pizza and beer are not a balanced meal, and that someone should probably clean the toilet once in a while.

WENDY: He doesn't clean the toilet?

JANE: He doesn't clean *anything*. I go to his place and spend the first thirty minutes cleaning, so I can stand to be there. Then we have sex. And all I can think while we're having sex is how long it's been since the sheets have been put through the wash, and I shouldn't be thinking that. And *why* am I thinking that. You didn't raise me to clean. I don't even know *how* to clean.
But I know you're supposed to wash sheets every few months, and I really don't think he does, so does that mean *I'm* the one who should clean the sheets, or does that mean I've succumbed to some gendered stereotype, when all I did, was come over to have sex?
It's my own fault.
I always fall for boys who never grow up.

WENDY: You inherited that from me.

JANE: Oh please. Dad was totally—

WENDY: I'm not talking about your dad.

JANE: I thought you and dad were college sweethearts?

WENDY: Yes…
But there was someone before him.

JANE: Mom! You never told me.

WENDY: I never told anyone.

JANE: Dad didn't know?

WENDY: He never asked.

JANE: Who is he? Where is he? Did he marry someone else? You need to find him! I'll Google him.

WENDY: Slow down. He—I doubt he's on the internet.

JANE: *Everyone's* searchable.

WENDY: I promise you, he's not.

JANE: You've checked.
While dad was alive?

WENDY: No. It's too complicated to explain.

JANE: Try me.
Oh…you had an affair.

WENDY: No!
He's just…
He's not reachable, unless you really want him. Then you can find him.

JANE: Is he, like, C I A or something?
You dated a SPY!

WENDY: You have a wild imagination.
I love that about you.

JANE: If you love him, why not reach out to him. See if he's been carrying the same torch all these years.

WENDY: Find out if he ever grew up.

JANE: It would be nice to know if they ever grow up.

(Beat)

WENDY: You don't have to marry him, Jane. You have options.

JANE: Every time I go to make the appointment, I start to wonder what this cluster of cells could turn into if I let it.
Would it be an uptight asshole, like John?
Or a mess, like Michael?
Or the family freak, like me?

Every part of me knows that I should just — take care of it—get rid of it. I'm not ready to have a kid. And I totally know it's my right to not let this thing freeload off of me for the next nine months until it becomes a human.

But this cell cluster—

This is a different cell cluster than the one I yell, and chant, and march about.

This is *my* cell cluster. My D N A.

Mine to screw up, or get right.

WENDY: Usually both, at the same time.

JANE: I don't know what to do, Mom.

WENDY: Don't look to me.

It's your decision.

JANE: But what would you do if you were in my shoes.

WENDY: I was in your shoes—a few times.

JANE: So you'd have the baby.

WENDY: I didn't say that.

JANE: Did you ever think—I mean this is weird because I'm standing right here, but since I wasn't planned…

Did you and Dad ever think about—

WENDY: Not your dad.

JANE: But you thought about it.

WENDY: I thought about it with all three of you.

Every time I found out I was pregnant, I thought about the one I hadn't had.

(*Off* JANE's *look:*)

WENDY: Surprised?

JANE: Um. Yeah.

Before John?

WENDY: Yes.

JANE: With Dad?

WENDY: No. A professor of mine—who was married.
And I didn't love him anyway.
And I knew I didn't want children.

JANE: Did Dad know?

WENDY: He knew there had been others before him.

JANE: Did he know you didn't want kids?

WENDY: Your dad was very charming. Somehow he
convinced me I would grow to love being a mom, and
a wife.

JANE: Did you?

WENDY: I grew to like having a family, and getting to
know each of you, but the mom part…
I wasn't cut out for it.
At least not the type of mom your dad thought I
should be.

JANE: I don't think I'm cut out to be a mom either.

WENDY: And that's your decision to make. No one
else's.
Not mine, or the man-boy who impregnated you.

JANE: I don't want to give up my life for a baby.

WENDY: Then don't.
My darling Jane, please don't.

JANE: But what if this is *exactly* what I'm supposed
to do with my life? What if this thing inside me is
supposed to cure Cancer or something?

WENDY: And what if it's just a baby?

JANE: That would be okay too. As long as she grows to
be strong, and smart, loyal, kind, fearless, and hopeful,
and passionate, and political, and ambitious, and
rebellious, and curious, and imaginative, and generous,
and sensitive, and honorable, and original—

WENDY: All of that is possible, if you live your life that way too.

And sometimes it's possible even if you don't.

Just look in the mirror.

You can do this Jane. Only if you want to.

JANE: What do you think I should do?

WENDY: When you were born, I made a promise that I would never make a decision for you that you were capable of making on your own.

But I will say this.

You are exactly the type of woman who should be raising a daughter.

(Another wall of the house falls away.)

(Transition)

Another Afterthought

(WENDY steps into a pool of light.)

(The clock stops ticking.)

WENDY: Once upon a time,

No. Not, "once upon a time…"

Now. Here.

I wonder if my mother read me that story of the little girl with my name as a cautionary tale.

Maybe she didn't have the words to warn me…

Perhaps it was *her* story and she felt better about passing on her warning in the context of a fictional narrative.

No, no. The truth is…

I think it's my story.

I believe it happened to me.

I believe I followed a boy who was full of promises, to a far off land.

But when we got there, he wasn't the boy who

had climbed through my window with stories of
adventures.
And no matter how magical that place was,
All I could see was the real him. And the lie.
So I left that place behind.
I told my mother about this place.
And her response was to tell my father…
Who said, "Wendy's imagination has gone wild again.
We must put a stop to it."
And so off to school I went.
A school for "young ladies"
Where we only learned how to be in service to
someone—*anyone* other than ourselves.
And where I began to suspect my dreams would never
be anything more than the nagging feeling that I had
forgotten something very important to me.
My schooling was effective.
It eradicated my dreams,
And replaced them with the desire to belong to
someone.
And so it happened again.
Another boy. Another far off land. This time Seattle.
He promised a lovely house, children, financial
stability, and the freedom to do anything I wanted…
…as long as I could manage the house and the
children,
which didn't leave much time for freedom.
I thought he was offering me a pedestal,
But it turned out to be a cage.
What if I went back to that first far away land?
Knowing what I know.
Having lived that life.
Back to the *place*. Not the boy.
The place with no boundaries.
No expectations.

The place where rules don't exist,
And possibilities are abundant.
I wouldn't be in the house cooking, cleaning, and
mending this time.
I'd be out with the boys! Getting dirty. Wrestling
crocodiles, and stealing pirate ships!
Sounds marvelous!

(Transition)

Wendy And Michael

(WENDY *and* MICHAEL *are putting the finishing touches on
a magnificent fort in the living room.)*

(The clock…well, you know.)

(MICHAEL *is in adult size footy pajamas because, why not?)*

WENDY: I'm glad you didn't think this was a crazy
idea. I couldn't stand the thought of leaving the house
without making one more fort.

MICHAEL: We better make it a good one.

WENDY: How long has it been?

MICHAEL: My twelfth birthday.
Dad came downstairs and said if I wanted to build a
tent he was signing me up for boy scouts.

WENDY: You cried—*begging* him not to.

MICHAEL: There are wolves, and bears, and things that
eat you.
Why would I build a fort in the woods when this one is
perfectly safe?

WENDY: I tried to get the twins to build a fort with me
last time they were here but they didn't understand
why we'd build one when there was already a roof on
the house.

MICHAEL: Those girls are so weird.

(The continue securing the fort to what remains of boxes and furniture.)

WENDY: I love that you decided to become an actor.
It's like playing pretend as a kid wasn't enough.
Are you happy?

MICHAEL: Yeah. I guess. I mean, I love being an actor, but…
You get typed into this *one thing* that the casting people decide you play,
And you know you can play like, fifty things, but they've made up their mind.
And that's it.
That's why I like doing the kids birthday parties.
It's not Ibsen, but it's also not Gangster #2 again.
I can walk into a party and tell the kids,
"I'm a wizard and I've come to cast a spell on you."
And the kids just go with it.
There's no hesitation.
No six year-old has ever said to me, "You're only five-ten and everyone knows a Wizard is over six feet."
They're just like, "You're a wizard! YAY!"

WENDY: When do we lose that?

(The last piece of the fort is put in place.)

MICHAEL: Okay. There we go.
So…who do you want to be?

WENDY: If I only knew…

MICHAEL: How about the one where we're camping, and get attacked by a grizzly bear?

WENDY: John's not here to play the bear.

MICHAEL: What about the one where we're children left in the forest, and we're raised by monkeys!

WENDY: I don't think my back can take that one anymore.

MICHAEL: Okay. Ummmmmmm......

WENDY: Michael, do you know the story of the girl who could fly?

MICHAEL: I don't think so.

WENDY: No one ever told you about the crocodile? The mermaids?
The second star to the right?

MICHAEL: This sounds exciting.

WENDY: Pretend you're asleep.

(MICHAEL *lays down, and fake snores.* WENDY *opens a window and climbs on the sill.*)

WENDY: Psst. Boy! Boy!

MICHAEL: *(Pretends to wake up)* Who's there?

WENDY: Wendy!

MICHAEL: That's my mother's name!

WENDY: I'm a different Wendy. I come from a land far, far away from here, where children laugh and play all day, and never forget how to have fun.

MICHAEL: Amazing!

WENDY: Would you like to come with me?

MICHAEL: I would!

WENDY: All you have to do is think good thoughts, which shouldn't be hard, because you have lived a very privileged life.

MICHAEL: Okay! Ummmmmm.
Candy, ice cream, video games.

WENDY: Dig deeper!

MICHAEL: Going barefoot, lighting farts on fire, double pepperoni pizza, finding five dollars on the street, winning call in contests on the radio, movie popcorn, flannel sheets, energy drinks, when mom does my laundry, happy hour, flip flops, skinny dipping, ig-pay atin-lay, finding a stray dog, cereal milk, sour candy, drive in burger joints...

Why isn't it working?

WENDY: It will! Keep going!

MICHAEL: Good weed, unprotected sex, Comi-con, baseball cards, skipping rocks, s'mores, Green Day, My Little Pony, illegal fireworks, warm slippers, free porn, bonfires, all-day breakfast, nude beaches, sleeping 'till noon, negative S T D tests, dinosaurs, cartoons—

WENDY: You're almost there!

MICHAEL: Personal artistic fulfillment!!!!

(And like that, MICHAEL and WENDY are flying. The lights are magical. The stars are magnificent. Maybe there's even a magical sound effect.)

MICHAEL: It worked!

WENDY: I told you it would. Now, shall we go?

MICHAEL: Go where?

WENDY: We wanna head toward those stars—

MICHAEL: But what about John and Jane? We can't leave them.

WENDY: Forget them. Come with me where you'll never, never have to worry about grown up things again.

MICHAEL: Never is an awfully long time.
Can't we come back for them someday?

WENDY: We can...
Or we can run away and be happy without them.

(MICHAEL *breaks "character" and instantly falls to the ground. There is nothing magical about the living room anymore.*)

MICHAEL: Wait, are we talking for real right now, or—

WENDY: I don't know.

MICHAEL: Because you told me I had to find a place to live.

WENDY: I don't know.

MICHAEL: But mom—

WENDY: I don't know!

MICHAEL: The thought of you going away makes me very upset.

WENDY: Oh baby, I could never go away from you forever.
Maybe just a short trip.
However long it takes to find myself.

MICHAEL: But you're right here.

WENDY: I haven't been here for a very long time.

MICHAEL: What did we do to make you regret being our mom?
We were good kids.
And now you're running away from us.

WENDY: Not from you.
From the person I never meant to be.

MICHAEL: We have a good life!

WENDY: But it's not the life I wanted.
It's merely the life I chose.
Or was chosen for me.
I can't even remember anymore.

MICHAEL: I don't understand the difference.

WENDY: Oh, Michael. My sweet, sweet Michael.

Do you know why you and your brother are so different?

MICHAEL: Because he's a jerk-face.

WENDY: Because when I saw how serious he was, I knew I had already messed him up. I vowed you would grow up to love your life, and to know how to laugh. I hoped you would retain your childlike sense of wonder long after childhood had passed you by.
And I succeeded.
You are everything I wanted you to be.
But that's also how I failed you.
You have no practical skills. No sense of responsibility. No follow through. You see life in the 14-hour chunks of time you are awake, rather than the 80-year journey that we're all on.
Your list of good thoughts was juvenile—
Pathetic really.

MICHAEL: Don't be mean.

WENDY: I'm not saying it to be mean.
But…maybe, darling—
It's time to grow up.

MICHAEL: I don't wanna grow up!
I like myself.

WENDY: You're a child. In a man's body. In footy pajamas.

MICHAEL: They're cozy.

WENDY: I wanted more for you than timecards, business meetings, and mortgages. But I never asked you what you wanted.

MICHAEL: I don't want them.

WENDY: But how do you know?

MICHAEL: I just do.

I see John's life and want the opposite.
I want to create things.
I want to feel things.
I want to live my life with reckless abandon.
And yeah, that might mean I'm screwed at some point.
But knowing I've lived is far better than playing it safe.
I'm not interested in fear.
And you shouldn't be either.
Life is too wonderful.
(He jumps up on the couch, to flying position.)
I will go with you!

(The magic doesn't return. MICHAEL *jumps off the couch and runs to the open window.)*

MICHAEL: I WILL GO WITH YOU WENDY!!!!!!

*(*WENDY *jumps on the couch, flying position. The magic returns!)*

WENDY: You see the two stars?

MICHAEL: Yes!

WENDY: Head towards the second one to the right.

MICHAEL: Then what?

WENDY: Straight on 'til—

(Suddenly a ship CAPTAIN *[*JOHN*] climbs through the window.)*

CAPTAIN: Arrrrrrg! A new boy!

MICHAEL: Who is that?

CAPTAIN: I'm the ol' ship captain and it's my sky you be travlin' in.

MICHAEL: There are no ships in the sky!

CAPTAIN: Of course there arrrrr. An' I'm takin' you back with me, where you'll scrub the floors, and peel the taters.

I'm gonna give you a work ethic, boy. And if yer naughty, you'll walk the plank!

(CAPTAIN *grabs* MICHAEL *and ties him to a chair.*)

MICHAEL: Wendy!

(WENDY *appears. Sword drawn. Ready for battle*)

WENDY: Not so fast Captain! Release the boy!

CAPTAIN: What's this? A *girl* thinks she can defeat the Captain!

WENDY: Is that crazier than a Captain thinking he can defeat a girl?

CAPTAIN: That's how it works in the other stories!

WENDY: This is a new story! A *better* story! En garde!

(*An EPIC sword fight takes place. Over furniture. Under tables. Around boxes. Swinging from the chandelier. Whatever your set can do, DO IT!*)

(CAPTAIN *and* WENDY *should gain and lose control equally. But she should always gain it back in a clever way.*)

(*Eventually...*)

WENDY: I need back up!

MICHAEL: I can't get free!

WENDY: Oh sweetie, I didn't mean you.
(*Calling*)
BELLE!!!!!!

(*Enter* BELLE [JANE]. *She's a girly girl/ badass. No dainty tutu for her.*)

BELLE: Wendy!

WENDY: He's stronger than I remember.

CAPTAIN: From sucking the meat off little boys bones.

BELLE: I'll get Michael. You hold the Captain off.

*(Throughout this next section, WENDY and CAPTAIN
continue to battle, but the focus is on MICHAEL and BELLE)*

MICHAEL: You know my name?

BELLE: Of course I know your name.

MICHAEL: Who are you?

BELLE: Do you want to exchange pleasantries or should
I rescue you?

MICHAEL: You're pretty.
You look like my sister.
Which, now that I say that out loud…

BELLE: I may be pretty, but lucky for you
I'm also smart, industrious, and—
(Releasing him from his rope)
—great with knots.

MICHAEL: I always wanted my own manic pixie dream
girl.

BELLE: Oh, hell no. I'm not here to save your ass by
playing you an obscure song.
I'm here to give my girl Wendy some back up.

MICHAEL: But you make me feel things I've never felt
before.
I'm in love with you.
Like massively.

BELLE: We'll get you into therapy as soon as we kill the
Captain.

MICHAEL: Kill him?! I thought this was supposed to be
fun and games.

BELLE: It is!

MICHAEL: MOMMA!!!!!!!!

*(WENDY tosses BELLE her sword and BELLE takes over the
fight. WENDY rushes down to MICHAEL.)*

WENDY: You okay?

MICHAEL: I wanna go home. I don't like this story after all. We've never killed someone before.

WENDY: Michael! This is exactly like your video games.

MICHAEL: Except real!

WENDY: Yes! It's thrilling!

MICHAEL: This is scary.

WENDY: You just need a snack.

(WENDY *quickly goes to the kitchen and returns with a juice box and some cookies.* MICHAEL *takes them to the couch and curls into the fetal position, nibbling away, while the women wrap the battle up.)*

(Working together, they cleverly toss CAPTAIN *out the window. We hear him fall, splat.* WENDY *grabs the infernal clock from its place on the wall and tosses it down as well.)*

(A crocodile eats them up.)

BELLE: We did it!

WENDY: You were amazing!

BELLE: I only finished what you started!

WENDY: I feel so alive!

*(*BELLE *starts to climb out the window.)*

BELLE: Let's find another overconfident, mediocre man, and put him in his place!

*(*WENDY *starts to follow her out of the window.)*

MICHAEL: I want to go home.

*(*WENDY *turns to Michael, aware she has to make a decision right now—another adventure, or* MICHAEL.)

BELLE: He can't get home by himself?

WENDY: He doesn't know the way.

BELLE: He'll figure it out.

WENDY: He's not like the other boy.

BELLE: Thank goodness.

WENDY: Michael. I have to —
I need to go.
Please understand this.

MICHAEL: I *don't* understand.
We can have adventures here.

WENDY: Not the kind I want to have.

BELLE: Not the kind she deserves.

MICHAEL: *(To BELLE)* You stay out of this. And I don't
find you attractive anymore.

WENDY: Michael. Remember when you were a boy,
and you went away to summer camp, I always told
you to be brave?

MICHAEL: Uh, huh.

WENDY: I was really telling myself to be brave. I knew I
was going to miss you so much.
But I also knew that you were going to get to do
amazing things.
And that you would come home and we'd have a
million things to talk about.
As much as I wanted to keep you home with me, I
knew the right thing to do was to let you have your
adventure.
Do you understand what I'm saying?

(Pause. MICHAEL refuses to give an inch.)

WENDY: *(To BELLE)* Let me just take him back.

BELLE: You've waited long enough.

WENDY: So what's a few more days?

BELLE: Promise you'll come back soon.

WENDY: I will try.
You see, I have commitments…

BELLE: Don't forget the one to yourself.
(And with that she departs through the window, and with her, all the magic.)

(WENDY goes to MICHAEL.)

WENDY: It was supposed to be fun.

MICHAEL: I was scared.

WENDY: So am I.

MICHAEL: Then stop this nonsense. Don't sell the house. Don't leave me all alone. Stay here and be my mother.

WENDY: I love you Michael. And I'll always be your mother. But I need to be other things too.
I want to show you the woman I could have been.
The woman I'm going to be.
But I need you to let me go.

(MICHAEL throws his empty juice box across the floor and turns his back to WENDY.)

(This kills her, but eventually she gets up and stands on the couch, in flying position.)

WENDY: And Wendy assured Michael,
(In "character" again)
I must go, for I have been sent a message, from a strong and powerful wind. She told me, "This is your journey. You must go it alone, and without fear." But one day I will return and tell you about my adventures, and you will tell me about yours.

MICHAEL: I *hate* adventures.

(Pause. When she's ready…)

WENDY: And even though she was hurting the ones she loved, Wendy knew she was making the best decision for herself.

And so she flew away.

(The final wall of the house falls away, and with it any remnants of what was once in the house. Only an empty floor remains.)

(Transition)

Never Grow Up

(JOHN, JANE, and MICHAEL, in precisely that order, sit on the bare floor of their empty, wall-less house.)

(We hear the "cock-a-doodle-doo" of a rooster off in the distance.)

MICHAEL: This is…
Strange

JANE: It's like we never lived here.

JOHN: Like we'll cease to exist the minute we hand over the keys.

JANE: Goodbye house.

MICHAEL: Don't say that. Goodbye means going away, and going away means forgetting.

(Beat)

JOHN: It looks exactly the way it did when we moved in.

MICHAEL: That first night—do you remember? The campout?
(For JANE's benefit)
The moving truck was late, so we got to camp out in the living room.

JOHN: Dad wanted to get a hotel—

MICHAEL: But mom said—

JOHN & MICHAEL: "It's time for an adventure."

MICHAEL: The first of many.
And now, no more.

JOHN: The house will be gone in a few days.

(A rooster crows.)

JANE: Since when are there roosters in this
neighborhood?

JOHN: It's those damn Millennials with their backyard
chickens.

JANE: Chickens don't crow.

MICHAEL: And *we're* Millennials. But we don't own
chickens.

(The rooster crows again.)

JOHN: I'm glad the developer didn't hear them when he
put in the offer.

*(The rooster crows once more. We hear WENDY run and
open a window upstairs.)*

WENDY: *(O S)* Cock-a-doodle-doo!

JOHN: Mother's gone mad.

JANE: No she hasn't.

MICHAEL: I've never heard her talk to roosters before.

JOHN: What if she doesn't leave?

What if her plan this entire time, was to be bulldozed
down with the house?

JANE: She's not suicidal, John.

JOHN: You don't know that.

(Beat)

MICHAEL: The house looks sad. Like it knows what's going to happen to it.

JOHN: Houses don't have feelings, Michael.

MICHAEL: This one does.
It's going to be okay, House.

(*Beat*)

JOHN: Technically speaking, the house is not going to be okay.

JANE: John!

JOHN: I don't want to *lie* to it if it has feelings.

MICHAEL: Are we going to be okay?

JANE: We don't have any other choice.

JOHN: It's time to grow up.
All of us.
Whether we want to or not.

MICHAEL: They don't talk about this part when you're a kid.
It's all, "you can be whatever you want to be."
But like really, it's actually, "Get a job. Pay bills. Watch your parents die, or fall apart right in front of your eyes."

JANE: Or both.

JOHN: Being an adult sucks.

JANE: I never thought I'd hear you admit that.

MICHAEL: So what are we going to do?

(*The children think for a moment.*)

JANE: I'm going to need you two around so...

JOHN: Did Jane just admit she needs a man's help?

MICHAEL: *Two* men.

JOHN: There *is* magic in this house!

JANE: What I mean is, if we all have to grow up, let's do it together.

John, just be our brother. Not our dad.

And Michael, you're gonna have to pull your weight.

And I—

I'll try to give you more credit, and stop giving you shit simply for being born with a Y chromosome.

(The rooster crows again. We hear steps on the roof. The children look up.)

JOHN: Not it.

        MICHAEL: Not it.

                JANE: Not—
                I hate you both.

(JANE stands, but before exiting, she runs back and pulls JOHN and MICHAEL into a bear hug pile on the floor. The children laugh together.)

(Transition)

The Unwriting

(JANE climbs on to the roof, and sits next to WENDY.)

JANE: How'd you get up here without breaking your neck?

WENDY: Yoga at the Y.

JANE: I should look into that.

WENDY: I hear it's good for pregnancy.
Are you still…?

JANE: Yeah. I'm gonna figure it out.
So, you can't, like disappear forever.

WENDY: I'm not going far.

(Beat)

JANE: John and Michael are downstairs. We all thought we'd come say goodbye to the house.

WENDY: That's nice of you.

JANE: John thinks you're going to jump.

WENDY: If I were going to kill myself, it wouldn't be here — leaving my ghost to wander the halls of the new condos for eternity.

JANE: Maybe if you told us your plan…

WENDY: I don't have a plan.

JANE: You must know something. Like where you're sleeping tonight?

WENDY: Jane, darling, you and your brothers can conspire and cajole all you want. But I'm not telling you where I'm going or what I'm doing. If I feel like checking in with you once I get there, I'll give you a ring. And if I don't, I won't.

JANE: But what if we need you?

WENDY: You'll be fine.

JANE: You don't know that.

WENDY: You'll figure out a way to be fine.

JANE: What if you need us?

WENDY: I won't.

JANE: Well, thanks.

WENDY: I'll always love you. I'll always think about you. But the days of needing someone, or someone needing me have passed.

JANE: We just want to make sure you're taken care of.

WENDY: You're putting the same limitations on me that your father did. And I'm through with all that. I'm through with—
(*Her voice catches*)

I'm doing my own thing now and—
One step at a time without him, and—

(WENDY *begins to cry. It's the first time we've seen her grief come out in this way.* JANE *moves over to her.*)

JANE: Mom.

Mom, it's okay.

WENDY: How is it possible to miss someone this much, when you spent forty-one years thinking about the day you'd finally get to be your own person?

JANE: You miss Dad?

WENDY: Of course I miss him. He was my husband. I loved him.

JANE: It's just—
For the last month you've been telling us that—

WENDY: Did you know your father and I—before we had you kids—we'd planned on living abroad. Our plan was to move to a new country, and just when we found ourselves getting too comfortable there, we'd pack up and move again.

JANE: That sounds incredible.

WENDY: It still might have been possible with one baby, but then Michael came before we knew it.
By the way, it is possible to get pregnant while breastfeeding. Don't know why I listened to that old wives tale.
Then your father thought it would be better to take a bank job. Insurance. A mortgage.
His head was looking towards the future.
Mine was in Berlin. Prague. Cologne.
And he knew it.
Whenever one of you kids was driving us mad, he'd look at me and say, "Amsterdam?"

JANE: I remember that.

WENDY: "Cairo?"

JANE: I always wondered what he meant.

WENDY: It meant, "let's get the hell out of here."
But we never did.
He thought it was enough to joke about it.

JANE: It's not too late. You could go now.

WENDY: I'm not as young as I used to be.

JANE: No one is.

WENDY: What I mean is… Time flies.
Differently than it flew when I was a little girl.
Or maybe I was the one who was flying, and time was
standing still.
(Beat)
Promise me you won't give up. And don't
compromise.
You've got so much life in front of you. Don't get to my
age and realize you never really lived.

JANE: You've lived a great life.

WENDY: Someone else's great life.
I'm sorry if it hurts you to hear that.

JANE: Deep down, I think I knew.

WENDY: Do you think your father knew? Do you think
his little jokes, "Venice, Barcelona?" were his way of
apologizing for keeping me here?
Or maybe he was telling me to run?

JANE: Doesn't really matter now, does it?

WENDY: I suppose not.

JANE: Can we get down from here? It's dangerous.

WENDY: You go. I want to look at the stars.

JANE: Let me at least get you a blanket.

WENDY: See, you're turning in to a mother already.

(JANE *starts to leave. But* WENDY *stops her.*)

WENDY: Jane?
You know that place between sleep and awake — that place where you still remember dreaming?

JANE: Yeah.

WENDY: That's where I'm going.

JANE: *(Doesn't get it)* Okay…

WENDY: You'll tell your brothers?

JANE: You tell them. Come down. It's freezing.
You can't stay up here all night.

WENDY: You should go home now. Be careful getting down.
I'll see you again soon, Jane.

(JANE *climbs down off the roof.*)

(WENDY *carefully gets to her feet.*)

WENDY: Going barefoot, warm towels fresh from the dryer, gardening, mani/pedi's, double pepperoni pizza, puppy breath, cooking shows, flannel sheets, lunch on the waterfront, a glass of Rosé, a *bottle* of Rosé, the smell of rain, a thunderstorm, an oboe and cello duet, my children's faces, my husband's laugh…
(And she's flying)

(Transition)

Never Never Neverland

(A magical, wooded area, straight out of a Disney movie. Majestic trees surround the old floor of Wendy's house, and greenery shoots up from the planks. Vines made for swinging tempt us from every angle. The glow of fairies, and the songs of mermaids are not too far in the distance.)

(The rooster crows again, but this time much closer.)

(WENDY *emerges from the trees.*)

WENDY: Cock-a-doodle-doo!

(*A* BOY, *12, appears. He is NOT dressed like Peter Pan.
They meet on the old plank floors.*)

BOY: Cock-a-doodle-doo!

WENDY: You're still here!

BOY: Where else would I be?

WENDY: It's been such a long time. I thought you might
have—

BOY: You could have come sooner.
I taught you how to fly.

WENDY: I was busy.

BOY: What's "busy?"

WENDY: Nothing you need to worry about.

BOY: You look different.
(*He inspects her face.*)
What are those?

WENDY: Wrinkles.

BOY: They're soft! Where did they come from?

WENDY: Laughter at first.
Then stress.
Now, sorrow.

BOY: I love laughing.

WENDY: I don't remember how.

BOY: You used to laugh so hard it would make me
laugh even harder.

WENDY: I did?

BOY: Once I laughed so hard I farted.
Do you fart when you laugh?

WENDY: I don't think so.

(The BOY *does boy things like tossing rocks at trees, or making himself burp.)*

WENDY: You haven't changed much.

BOY: Nope!

WENDY: But you're as old as I am.

BOY: I'm twelve.

WENDY: Oh come on, you're at least sixty by now.

BOY: Am not!

WENDY: You must be.

BOY: You're stupid if you think that! I'm twelve and you're thirteen.

WENDY: I am not stupid!
How many thirteen year olds look like me?

BOY: Some of the boys are thirteen, but they don't have wrinkles. Maybe only girls get them.

WENDY: Maybe.

BOY: So why'd you finally come back?

WENDY: I wondered if you were still here.

BOY: 'Course I am.

WENDY: What have you been doing all these years?

BOY: Playing.
Making stuff. Breaking stuff.
Getting dirty.

WENDY: And that's enough for you?

BOY: What else is there?
What about you?

WENDY: Mostly I've been breaking stuff.

BOY: It's fun, right?

WENDY: Not always.

BOY: Where are John and Michael?

WENDY: You know about my kids?

BOY: Of course I do.

WENDY: Did they ever come here with you?

BOY: I never asked them to. We've got enough boys right now.
Plus they seem kind of…

WENDY: Go ahead.

BOY: The older one is mean, and the younger one cries a lot.

WENDY: They're under a lot of pressure.

BOY: What's "pressure"?

WENDY: Expectations.

BOY: Like how I always have to climb the trees in Capture the Flag 'cuz I'm the best at it?

WENDY: Kind of like that.

(BOY *stands.*)

BOY: I'm bored. Let's go find the boys.

WENDY: Am I too old to come back?

BOY: You're only thirteen.
We've been waiting for our mother.
Come on!

WENDY: Whoa. Wait a minute.

I don't want to be your mother.

BOY: Why not?

WENDY: I've been a mother. I want to be something else now.

BOY: You can't be a boy. We got enough boys.

You can't be a mermaid because you have feet.

WENDY: No, not a mermaid.
I want…

(Pause)

BOY: Well, whaddya want?

WENDY: I want to be Wendy.
Whatever that means.
Whoever she is.

BOY: But you'll still cook for us, right?
And my big toe sticks out of the hole in my—

WENDY: No. No, I won't do that for you.
Is that all you think I'm good for?

BOY: You were good at it before.

WENDY: But I'm more than that.
I can be so much more.

BOY: Whatever. We'll figure it out when we get home.

(BOY holds out his hand to WENDY.)

WENDY: I don't think I can.

BOY: Just think good thoughts.

WENDY: No.
I don't think I can stay here.

BOY: Sure you can.
(He takes her hand.)
You must. It's what I want.

(WENDY pulls her hand away from the BOY.)

WENDY: But it's not what I want.
Don't you see?
Go away. Pretend I never called for you.

BOY: You're hurting my feelings.

WENDY: And you're hurting mine!

I'm sorry I've wasted your time.
I—I really thought I wanted to come back.
To see who I could be here.
To wrestle with the crocodiles.
To swim with the mermaids.
But I...
And you—you never grew up.

BOY: I said I wouldn't, and I didn't.

WENDY: No, you didn't.
But I did.
And I want more than pirate ships now.
I want adventures that take me to places that are *real*.
Where I can swim with dolphins, and climb mountains,
and see the pyramids.
Where I can experience things that make me know
I'm...
That I'm not over yet.
That I've still got a long life ahead of me.
That who I was is still in me.
And she's been patiently waiting for me.

BOY: Whatever.
I'm outta here.
(He is off.)

*(WENDY looks around Never Neverland, until she sees
the audience. Really sees them. Maybe she's even in the
audience by the time she notices them. This story is for
them.)*

WENDY: Once upon a time...
What does that mean anyway?
"Once upon a time."
What time?
It's important to know exactly when.
It offers perspective.
Context.

This story is *now*.
And my story did not happen "once"
There are many women who—
Maggie, three doors down. She wanted to be a nurse.
But her husband travels for work, and her daughter
needed someone home, so her dreams were put aside.
And Rose. Twice a week we walk the track at the Y.
She has her Doctorate in Victorian Literature. Can
you imagine? But her husband's salary is three times
what Rose's was as a professor, so when her husband's
mother needed full time care…
Are you sensing a trend here?
Once upon a time,
I asked my husband why he didn't stay home with the
kids while *I* went to work.
He laughed. And it wasn't a chuckle.
It was a hearty, full-throated, belly-seizing laugh.
And then he picked up his briefcase, kissed me on the
cheek, and walked out the door.
And so…
How would I rewrite that story?
For my granddaughters.
For every little girl who will soon realize how their
gender will betray them.
What would get erased?
Perhaps the boy would never come.
Maybe there is no such thing as a far off land.
Instead Wendy would read, think, and discover the
world that already belonged to her.
And when her parents reminded her of her place, she
would tell them,
"There is no place big enough to contain me."
When she grew old enough to marry, she would only
settle for someone who understood that a house was a
cage to Wendy.

And together they would travel the world.
And ask each other challenging questions, just for the
sake of a good debate.
Perhaps one child would come along. But not three.
And though their love would remain solid, it was their
mutual respect and admiration for one another that
would grow beyond measure.
This is the story I will tell the girls.
This is the story I hope they will carry deep in their
hearts.
This is the story I will write.

(WENDY *leaves the theatre. She's got a lot of living to do.*)

(*Transition*)

An Afterthought

(JANE *sits in a rocking chair, holding a tightly bundled baby
girl.*)

(JOHN *and* MICHAEL *quietly enter.*)

MICHAEL: (*Almost whispering*) Knock, knock.

JANE: Hey. You just missed her awake.

JOHN: She's beautiful, Jane.

JANE: She's going to be a handful. There's an
indomitable spirit in this one.

MICHAEL: Need us to do anything? I'm getting better at
laundry. And I'm a master of ordering take out.

JANE: A few minutes of adult conversation would be
nice.

JOHN: So her father…?

JANE: —Wants to stay a boy. (*To the baby*) We don't
have time for that, do we Molly?

MICHAEL: And no word from—

JANE: No.

MICHAEL: I really thought she'd come back when Molly was born.

JOHN: *(No anger)* Or at least call.

JANE: She sent a gift.

MICHAEL: She did?

(JANE *pulls out an all white, bound book, its pages blank.*)

JOHN: A blank book?

JANE: There's an inscription.

(MICHAEL *flips to the page.*)

MICHAEL: *(Reading)* To my wild, imaginative, daring, granddaughter: May your many adventures fill these pages. Love, Wendy.

JOHN: Wendy.

JANE: She's reclaiming herself.

MICHAEL: Was there a return address?

JANE: Nepal.

JOHN: It's kind of a useless gift. An infant can't fill it with stories.

JANE: I will do it for her, until she's ready to do it herself.

MICHAEL: What kind of stories?

JANE: Well…
This is one of her favorites.
Once upon a time…
There was a girl.

MICHAEL: Is it Molly?

JANE: Just listen.

(MICHAEL *settles in for the story. It takes* JOHN *a little while longer, but eventually he too settles around the rocking chair for story time.*)

JANE: And the girl knew she was capable of great things. She knew this because when she put her mind to it, she had moved mountains. She had quieted storms and calmed choppy seas. She knew her strength did not have to be compromised for vulnerability, for she contained multitudes of powers within her.

One day, the girl grew very, very sad because she felt she had lost her self.

And though she longed for great adventures, the girl knew she had to find her self, before she did anything else.

So off she went.

She journeyed for many years, but only seemed to get farther from her self.

(WENDY *appears somewhere in the story.*)

WENDY: I don't even know where I am anymore. I don't even know *who* I am.

JANE: Eventually she came across three spirits in the woods. The spirits were familiar to her, as though she had created them within her.

They asked,

"Are you lost?"

WENDY: Yes. Yes, I am very lost.

JANE: What do you seek?

WENDY: My self.

JANE: And what do you need your self for?

WENDY: To feel complete again. To feel as though I matter. To know I exist.

To know I haven't been erased, or worse, never written at all.

JANE: The spirits took pity on her, though she asked
for no pity. Before she realized it, they surrounded her,
and one by one they reminded her—
You are full of joy.
You are full of patience.

MICHAEL: You are playful.

JOHN: You are strong.

JANE: You are smart.

MICHAEL: You are whimsy.

JOHN: You are kindness.

JANE: You are hope.

MICHAEL: You are a bright umbrella in a relentless rain.

JOHN: You are a song with a melody, that begs to be
sung.

JANE: You are the rogue flower growing up from the
pavement.

MICHAEL: You are my heartbeat.

JOHN: You are my wisdom.

JANE: You are love.

And you are loved.

WENDY: I never knew anyone could see these things in
me.

JANE: But the spirits assured her,

JANE & MICHAEL & JOHN: We see them.

WENDY: Then I am complete.
And I can be on my way.

JANE: "Wait!" The spirits called.
You didn't tell us your name.

WENDY: I—
(Deep breath)

I AM WENDY!

(Blackout)

END OF PLAY

www.ingramcontent.com/pod-product-compliance
Lightning Source LLC
Chambersburg PA
CBHW052218090426
42741CB00010B/2588